If you could change something about how you said goodbye to dad what would it be?

_____

_____

_____

_____

_____

_____

_____

_____

_____

_____

_____

_____

_____

_____

_____

_____

_____

How do you feel about dad not being around anymore?

What funny story did dad tell you that made you happy?

Are you still doing all the things dad taught you to do?

What does dad's voice sound like?

What did dad and you like doing the most together?

What did you wish you could have said to dad more often when he was alive?

What did dad say he liked the most about you?

What do you talk to grandma or grandpa about after dad's death?

Did you have a nickname for dad?

What do you talk to mom about after dad's death?

What was dad's favourite snack to eat?

What did dad and you like to do during the spring season?

What favourite snack did dad get or made for you?

How have your friends supported you after dad's death?

What did people say they liked the most about dad?

What did dad say you should do when he died?

Do you remember what favourite clothing dad liked to wear?

Do you remember what favourite shoe dad liked to wear?

Did dad like any sport and if he did, was he good at it?

What did you promise dad you will continue to do when he died?

What music did dad liked to listen to the most?

What did dad and you like to do during the summer season?

What did dad and you like to do during the winter season?

What was the nickname dad gave to you?

What type of drink did he like the most?

Do you remember dad's favourite hobby?

Write down dad's favourite food?

When dad was ill at the hospital or at home, how did it make you feel?

What did dad do a lot that made you laugh?

What did dad and you like to do during the fall season?

Write down your favourite memory of dad?

How did you feel when dad was getting buried?

_____

_____

_____

_____

_____

_____

_____

_____

_____

_____

_____

_____

_____

_____

_____

_____

How are things been with your siblings since dad is no longer around?

What would you like dad to know about in the afterlife that you are proud of doing now?

_____

_____

_____

_____

_____

_____

_____

_____

_____

_____

_____

_____

_____

_____

_____

_____

_____

_____

_____

_____

Have you been feeling differently without dad being around?

What gift did you give to dad that he was really happy to receive?

How are things been with mom since dad is no longer around?

What did dad say about the afterlife?

What would you like to tell dad that you didn't get a chance to say to him?

Made in the USA
Columbia, SC
05 January 2020